HISTORY'S MOST INFLUENTIAL
WOMEN

FROM THE Mid-1900s TO THE Late 1900s

Lucille Ball to Diana, Princess of Wales

EDITED BY KATHLEEN KUIPER

IN ASSOCIATION WITH

Published in 2024 by Britannica Educational Publishing
(a trademark of Encyclopædia Britannica, Inc.)
in association with Rosen Educational Services, LLC
2544 Clinton Street, Buffalo, NY 14224.

Copyright © 2024 Encyclopædia Britannica, Inc. Britannica, Encyclopædia Britannica, and the Thistle logo are registered trademarks of Encyclopædia Britannica, Inc. All rights reserved.

Rosen Educational Services materials copyright © 2024 Rosen Educational Services, LLC. All rights reserved.

Distributed exclusively by Rosen Educational Services.
For a listing of additional Britannica Educational Publishing titles, call toll free (800) 237-9932.

First Edition

Britannica Educational Publishing
Michael I. Levy: Executive Editor
Marilyn L. Barton: Senior Coordinator, Production Control
Steven Bosco: Director, Editorial Technologies
Lisa S. Braucher: Senior Producer and Data Editor
Yvette Charboneau: Senior Copy Editor
Kathy Nakamura: Manager, Media Acquisition
Kathleen Kuiper: Manager, Arts and Culture

Editor: Kathleen Kuiper
Book design: Michael Flynn

Photo credits: Cover https://commons.wikimedia.org/wiki/File:Elizabeth_II_in_Berlin_2015.JPG; p. 7 https://commons.wikimedia.org/wiki/File:LDBALL1950s.jpg; p. 11 https://commons.wikimedia.org/wiki/File:Young_Jiang_Qing_and_Mao3.jpg; p. 18 https://commons.wikimedia.org/wiki/File:Indira_Gandhi_official_portrait.png; p. 30 https://commons.wikimedia.org/wiki/File:AnneFrankSchoolPhoto.jpg; p. 44 https://commons.wikimedia.org/wiki/File:Billie_Jean_King_%C2%A9Lynn_Gilbert_1978.jpg; p. 57 Everett Collection/Shutterstock.com.

Cataloging-in-Publication Data

Names: Kuiper, Kathleen.
Title: From the mid-1900s to the late 1900s—Lucille Ball to Diana, Princess of Wales / edited by Kathleen Kuiper.
Description: New York : Britannica Educational Publishing, in Association with Rosen Educational Services. 2024. | Series: History's most influential women | Includes glossary and index.
Identifiers: ISBN 9781641900812 (library bound) | ISBN 9781641900805 (pbk) | ISBN 9781641900829 (ebook)
Subjects: LCSH: Women--Biography--Juvenile literature. | Women--History--20th century--Juvenile literature. | Women--History--Juvenile literature.
Classification: LCC HQ1123.K87 2024 | DDC 920.72 B--dc23

Manufactured in the United States of America

CPSIA Compliance Information: Batch #CWBRIT24. For further information contact Rosen Publishing at 1-800-237-9932.

CONTENTS

Introduction...........................4
Lucille Ball..........................6
Rosa Parks............................8
Jiang Qing...........................10
Elizabeth Stern......................13
Sirimavo R. D. Bandaranaike..........14
Indira Gandhi........................16
Eva Perón............................19
Rosalind Franklin....................21
Rosalyn S. Yalow.....................22
Nadine Gordimer......................24
Elizabeth II.........................25
Anne Frank...........................28
Violeta Barrios de Chamorro..........31
Sandra Day O'Connor..................32
Ellen Johnson Sirleaf................34
Gro Harlem Brundtland................36
Wangari Maathai......................37
Martha Stewart.......................39
Christiane Nüsslein-Volhard..........41
Billie Jean King.....................43
Mary Robinson........................45
Aung San Suu Kyi.....................47
Shirin Ebadi.........................50
Hillary Rodham Clinton...............52
Oprah Winfrey........................56
Rigoberta Menchú.....................59
Diana, Princess of Wales.............60
Glossary.............................62
For More Information.................63
Index................................64

Introduction

"What people see as fearlessness is really persistence."
—*Wangari Maathai (1940–2011)*

The world is filled with fascinating women, and each woman has her own compelling story. This book contains profiles of striking individuals who serve as outstanding representatives of their gender. It covers many of the most noteworthy, influential women from around the globe who lived between the mid-1900s and the late 1900s.

Some of these women have left their mark on humankind's collective creative history. A star of stage and screen in her own right, Lucille Ball is perhaps best known as the star of the *I Love Lucy* television program. Ball made people laugh as one of the world's greatest comic actors. More than that, she was a shrewd businessperson who became one of the first women to run a major Hollywood production company.

Many of the women in this book are world leaders, politicians, or monarchs. Queen Elizabeth II, who served as queen of England for 70 years, is one such leader. She came to the throne when she was 25 years old. Elizabeth was connected to another notable women profiled in this book, Diana, Princess of Wales. Diana's personality, beauty, and unwavering support of the arts, children's issues, and AIDS relief quickly made her a popular public figure all over the world. Her untimely death in 1997 at the age of 36 was mourned by many.

Other countries around the world also have been led by women in the modern age. The first female prime minister in history was Sirimavo Bandaranaike, elected to lead Sri Lanka in 1960. She would ultimately go on to serve three terms in that office, remaining an important part of

Sri Lankan politics until her death. Six years later, Indira Gandhi became the first female prime minister of India. She served four terms before being assassinated in 1984. Ireland elected its first female president, Mary Robinson, in 1990, and in 2006, Ellen Johnson Sirleaf became the first woman to be head of state in an African country when she was elected president of Liberia.

While the United States has yet to elect a woman president, there have been women who have achieved high political office and run for president. Among them is Hillary Rodham Clinton, who made political history as the first American first lady to win an elective office when she became a United States senator in 2001. Although her bid for president failed in 2008, Clinton earned her way back into the White House as secretary of state in Barack Obama's administration. Clinton's presidential campaign in 2016 brought her closer to achieving the presidency. Although she secured the popular vote, Clinton ultimately lost the election.

Most of the women in this book managed to flourish despite hardships. One striking example is Anne Frank. Her writings, published as *The Diary of a Young Girl*, portray her short life and insights as one of the millions of Jewish victims of the Holocaust. More than a classic of war literature, Anne Frank's diary puts a human face on an unimaginable tragedy, and serves as a beacon of hope to all young women who face adversity.

The influence of these women, and the others profiled in this book, reverberates throughout the ages. Their leadership, scientific research, and artistic vision have served to enrich, enlighten, and shape modern society. These amazing and influential individuals have given all of us, men and women alike, something to admire and strive for in our own lives.

LUCILLE BALL

(b. Aug. 6, 1911, Celoron, near Jamestown, N.Y., U.S.—d. April 26, 1989, Los Angeles, Calif.)

The radio and motion-picture actress Lucille Ball (in full Lucille Désirée Ball) was a longtime comedy star of American television, best remembered for her classic television comedy series *I Love Lucy*.

Ball determined at an early age to become an actress and left high school at age 15 to enroll in a drama school in New York City. Her early attempts to find a place in the theater all met with rebuffs, and she took a job as a model under the name Diane Belmont. She was moderately successful as a model. A poster on which she appeared brought her to the attention of the Hollywood studios and won her spots in *Roman Scandals* (1933), *Blood Money* (1933), *Kid Millions* (1934), and other movies.

Ball remained in Hollywood and appeared in increasingly larger roles in a succession of movies—*Carnival* (1935), *Stage Door* (1937), *Room Service* (1938), *Five Came Back* (1939). In 1940, she starred in *Too Many Girls*, which also featured the popular Cuban bandleader and actor Desi Arnaz, whom she married in 1940. For 10 years they conducted separate careers, he as a bandleader and she as a movie actress who was usually seen in B-grade comedies. She won major roles in *The Big Street* (1942) with Henry Fonda, *Du Barry Was a Lady* (1943), *Without Love* (1945), *Ziegfeld Follies* (1946), and *Sorrowful Jones* (1949) and *Fancy Pants* (1950), both with Bob Hope. All of her comedies were box office successes, but they failed to make the most of her wide-ranging talents.

In 1950 Ball and her husband formed Desilu Productions, which, after experimenting with a radio program, launched in October 1951 a television comedy series entitled *I Love Lucy*. Starring the two of them in a comedy version

Lucille Ball paved the way for future generations of female comedians, producers, and studio heads.

of their real lives, the show was an instant hit. For the six years (1951–56 and, under the title *The Lucille Ball-Desi Arnaz Show*, 1957–58) during which fresh episodes were produced, it remained at or near the top of the TV ratings. *I Love Lucy* proved to be an outstanding vehicle for Ball's exceptional comedic talents. As the character Lucy, a wisecracking housewife who regularly concocted schemes to get herself out of the house, Ball showcased her expertise for timing, physical comedy, and range of characterization. The show also introduced several technical innovations to television broadcasting (notably the use of three cameras to film the show) and set the standard for situation comedies, thriving in reruns for decades.

Meanwhile, Desilu acquired RKO Pictures, began producing other shows for television, and became one of the major companies in a highly competitive field. Ball and Arnaz were divorced in 1960. Two years later she succeeded him as president of Desilu, becoming the only woman at that time to lead a major production company.

After starring in the Broadway show *Wildcat* in 1961, Ball returned to television in *The Lucy Show* (1962–68). She resumed movie work with *Yours, Mine and Ours* (1968) and *Mame* (1974). In 1967, she sold Desilu and formed her own company, Lucille Ball Productions, which produced her third television series, *Here's Lucy* (1968–74). She continued to appear thereafter in special productions and as a guest star. In 1985, she played a Manhattan bag lady in the television film *Stone Pillow*. Her fourth television series, *Life with Lucy*, aired for two months in 1986.

ROSA PARKS

(b. Feb. 4, 1913, Tuskegee, Ala., U.S.—d. Oct. 24, 2005, Detroit, Mich.)

The African American civil rights activist Rosa Parks refused to relinquish her seat on a public bus to a white man, precipitating the 1955–56 Montgomery bus boycott in Alabama. Her act is recognized as the spark that ignited the U.S. civil rights movement.

In 1932, Rosa Louise McCauley married Raymond Parks, who encouraged her to return to high school and earn a diploma. She later made her living as a seamstress. In 1943, Rosa Parks became a member of the Montgomery chapter of the National Association for the Advancement of Colored People (NAACP), and she served as its secretary until 1956. On December 1, 1955, she was arrested for refusing to give her bus seat to a white man, a violation of the city's racial segregation ordinances.

Under the aegis of the Montgomery Improvement Association and the leadership of the young pastor of the Dexter Avenue Baptist Church, Martin Luther King Jr., a boycott of the municipal bus company was begun on December 5. (African Americans constituted some 70 percent of the ridership.) On November 13, 1956, the U.S. Supreme Court upheld a lower court's decision declaring Montgomery's segregated seating unconstitutional, and the court order was served on December 20; the boycott ended the following day. For her role in igniting the successful campaign, which brought King to national prominence, Parks became known as the "mother of the civil rights movement."

In 1957, Parks moved to Detroit, where, from 1965 to 1988, she was a member of the staff of Michigan Congressman John Conyers Jr. She also remained active in the NAACP. The Southern Christian Leadership Conference established the annual Rosa Parks Freedom Award in her honor. In 1987, she cofounded the Rosa and Raymond Parks Institute for Self Development to provide career training for young people. She was the recipient of numerous awards, including the Presidential Medal of Freedom (1996) and the Congressional Gold Medal (1999).

JIANG QING

(b. March 1914, Zhucheng, Shandong province, China—d. May 14, 1991)

Jiang Qing, born Li Jinhai, was the third wife of Chinese communist leader Mao Zedong and the most influential woman in the People's Republic of China for a while until her downfall in 1976, after Mao's death. As a member of the Gang of Four she was convicted in 1981 of "counter-revolutionary crimes" and imprisoned.

Jiang became a member of a theatrical troupe in 1929. Her activity in a communist-front organization in 1933 led to her arrest and detainment. Upon her release she went to Shanghai. She was arrested again in 1934 and left for Beijing after her release, but she later returned to Shanghai, where she played minor roles for the left-wing Diantong Motion Pictures Company under the name Lan Ping.

When the Japanese attacked Shanghai in 1937, Jiang fled to the Chinese Nationalist wartime capital at Chongqing, where she worked for the government-controlled Central Movie Studio until she crossed the Nationalist lines. She went through Xi'an to join the communist forces in Yan'an and started to use the name Jiang Qing. While a drama instructor at the Lu Xun Art Academy, she met Mao for the first time when he gave a talk at the school. They were married in 1939 (technically, she was Mao's fourth wife; he had an arranged marriage in his youth but never acknowledged it). The marriage was criticized by many party members, especially since the woman whom Mao divorced (one of the few women to survive the communists' Long March of 1934–35) was then hospitalized in Moscow. Party leaders agreed to the marriage on condition that Jiang stay out of politics for the next 20 years.

After the establishment of the People's Republic of China in 1949, Jiang remained out of public view except to serve as Mao's hostess for foreign visitors or to sit on

Jiang Qing and Mao Zedong are seen here in this photograph from 1945.

various cultural committees. In 1963, however, she became more politically active, sponsoring a movement in the theatrical form *jingxi* (Peking opera) and in ballet aimed at infusing traditional Chinese art forms with proletarian themes. Jiang's cultural reform movement gradually grew into a prolonged attack on many of the leading cultural and intellectual figures in China and culminated in the Cultural Revolution that by 1966 had begun to sweep the country.

Jiang reached the height of her power and influence in 1966, winning renown for her fiery speeches to mass gatherings and her involvement with the radical young Red Guard groups of the revolution. One of the few people whom Mao trusted, she became the first deputy head of the Cultural Revolution and acquired far-reaching powers over China's cultural life. She oversaw the total suppression of many traditional cultural activities during the decade of the revolution. As the revolution's initial fervor waned in the late 1960s, however, so did Jiang's prominence. She reemerged in 1974 as a cultural leader and spokeswoman for Mao's new policy of "settling down."

Mao died on September 9, 1976, and the radicals in the party lost their protector. A month later, wall posters appeared attacking Jiang and three other radicals as the Gang of Four, and the attacks grew progressively more hostile. Jiang and the other members of the Gang of Four were soon afterward arrested. She was expelled from the Communist Party in 1977. In 1980–81 at her public trial as a member of the Gang of Four, Jiang was accused of fomenting the widespread civil unrest that had gripped China during the Cultural Revolution, but she refused to confess her guilt; instead, she denounced the court and the country's leaders. She received a suspended death sentence, but in 1983 it was commuted to life imprisonment. Her death in prison was officially reported as a suicide.

ELIZABETH STERN

(b. Sept. 19, 1915, Cobalt, Ont., Can.—d. Aug. 18, 1980, Los Angeles, Calif., U.S.)

The Canadian-born American pathologist Elizabeth Stern is noted for her work on the stages of a cell's progression from a normal to a cancerous state.

Stern received a medical degree from the University of Toronto in 1939 and the following year went to the United States, where she became a naturalized citizen in 1943. She received further medical training at the Pennsylvania Medical School and at the Good Samaritan and Cedars of Lebanon hospitals in Los Angeles. She was one of the first specialists in cytopathology, the study of diseased cells. From 1963 she was professor of epidemiology in the School of Public Health at the University of California, Los Angeles.

While at UCLA, Stern became interested in cervical cancer, and she began to focus her research solely on its causes and progression. The discoveries she made during this period led her to publish in 1963 what is believed to be the first case report linking a specific virus (herpes simplex virus) to a specific cancer (cervical cancer). For another phase of her research, she studied a group of more than 10,000 Los Angeles county women who were clients of the county's public family planning clinics.

In a 1973 article in the journal *Science*, Stern became the first person to report a definite link between the prolonged use of oral contraceptives and cervical cancer. Her research connected the use of contraceptive pills containing steroids with cervical dysplasia, which is often a precursor of cervical cancer. In her most noted work in this field, Stern studied cells cast off from the lining of the cervix and discovered that a normal cell goes through 250 distinct stages of cell progression before reaching an advanced stage of cervical cancer. This prompted the development of diagnostic techniques and screening instruments to detect the cancer in its early stages. Her research helped make cervical cancer, with its slow rate of metastasis, one of the types of cancer that can be successfully treated by prophylactic measures (i.e., excision of abnormal tissue).

Stern continued her teaching and research into the late 1970s, despite undergoing chemotherapy for stomach cancer. She died of the disease in 1980.

SIRIMAVO R. D. BANDARANAIKE
(b. April 17, 1916, Ratnapura, Ceylon [now Sri Lanka]—d. Oct. 10, 2000, Colombo, Sri Lanka)

Upon her party's victory in the 1960 Ceylon general election, Sirimavo Ratwatte Dias Bandaranaike became the world's first woman prime minister. She left office in 1965 but returned to serve two more terms (1970–77, 1994–2000) as prime minister. The family she founded with her late husband, S.W.R.D. Bandaranaike, rose to great prominence in Sri Lankan politics.

Born into a wealthy family, she married the politician Bandaranaike in 1940 and began to interest herself in social welfare. After her husband, who became prime minister in 1956, was assassinated in 1959, she was induced by his Sri Lanka Freedom Party (SLFP) to become the party's leader. The SLFP won a decisive victory at the general election in July 1960, and she became prime minister.

Bandaranaike carried on her husband's program of socialist economic policies, neutrality in international relations, and the active encouragement of the Buddhist religion and of the Sinhalese language and culture. Her government nationalized various economic enterprises and enforced a law making Sinhalese the sole official language. By 1964, a deepening economic crisis and the SLFP's coalition with the Marxist Lanka Sama Samaja Party ("Ceylon Socialist Party") had eroded popular support for her government, which was resoundingly defeated in the general election of 1965. In 1970, however, her socialist coalition, the United Front, regained power.

As prime minister, Bandaranaike pursued more radical policies. Her government further restricted free enterprise, nationalized industries, carried out land reforms, and promulgated a new constitution that created an executive presidency and made Ceylon into a republic named Sri Lanka. While reducing inequalities of wealth, Bandaranaike's socialist policies had once again caused economic stagnation, and her government's support of Buddhism and the Sinhalese language had helped alienate the country's large Tamil minority. The failure to deal with ethnic rivalries and economic distress led, in the election of July 1977, to the SLFP's retaining only 8 of the 168 seats in the National Assembly, and Bandaranaike was replaced as prime minister.

In 1980, the Sri Lanka parliament stripped Bandaranaike of her political rights and barred her from political office, but in 1986 President J. R. Jayawardene granted her a pardon that restored her rights. She ran unsuccessfully as the SLFP's candidate for president in 1988, and after regaining a seat in parliament in 1989 she became the leader of the opposition party.

Bandaranaike's children, in the meantime, had become major political figures within the SLFP. Her son, Anura P.S.D. Bandaranaike (b. 1949), was first elected to parliament in 1977 and had become the leader of the SLFP's right-wing faction by 1984. He was frustrated in his bid to become the party's leader, however, by his sister Chandrika Bandaranaike Kumaratunga (b. 1945), who held left-wing views and was favored by their mother for the leadership.

In response, Anura defected from the SLFP and joined the rival United National Party (UNP) in 1993.

Chandrika had been active in the SLFP before marrying the film actor Vijaya Kumaratunga in 1978, and after his assassination in 1988 she rejoined her mother's party. She soon came to head its left-wing faction, and a string of electoral victories propelled her to the leadership of an SLFP-based coalition that won the parliamentary elections of August 1994. Chandrika became prime minister, and in November of that year she won the presidential election over the UNP candidate. Chandrika appointed her mother, Sirimavo Bandaranaike, to serve as prime minister in her new government, which mounted a major military campaign against Tamil separatists in 1995. Failing health forced Bandaranaike to resign her post in August 2000. Shortly after voting in the October parliamentary elections, she suffered a heart attack and died.

INDIRA GANDHI
(b. Nov. 19, 1917, Allahabad, India—d. Oct. 31, 1984, New Delhi)

Indira Gandhi served as prime minister of India for three consecutive terms (1966–77) and a fourth term (1980–84). She was assassinated by Sikh extremists.

Indira Priyadarshini Nehru was the only child of Jawaharlal Nehru, the first prime minister of independent India. She attended Visva-Bharati University, West Bengal, and the University of Oxford, and in 1942 she married Feroze Gandhi (died 1960), a fellow member of the Indian National Congress (Congress Party). She was a member of the working committee of the ruling Congress Party from 1955, and in 1959 she was elected to the largely honorary post of party president. Lal Bahadur Shastri, who became prime minister in 1964, named her minister of information and broadcasting in his government.

On Shastri's sudden death in January 1966, Gandhi became leader of the Congress Party—and thus also prime minister—in a compromise between the right and left wings of the party. Her leadership, however, came under continual challenge from the right wing of the party, led by a former minister of finance, Morarji Desai. In the election of 1967 she won a slim majority and had to accept Desai as deputy prime minister. In 1971, however, she won a sweeping electoral victory over a coalition of conservative parties. Gandhi strongly supported East Bengal (now Bangladesh) in its secessionist conflict with Pakistan in late 1971, and India's armed forces achieved a swift and decisive victory over Pakistan that led to the creation of Bangladesh.

In March 1972, buoyed by the country's success against Pakistan, Gandhi again led her new Congress Party to a landslide victory in national elections. Shortly afterward, her defeated Socialist Party opponent charged that she had violated the election laws. In June 1975, the High Court of Allahabad ruled against her, which meant that she would be deprived of her seat in Parliament and would have to stay out of politics for six years. In response, she declared a state of emergency throughout India, imprisoned her political opponents, and assumed emergency powers, passing many laws limiting personal freedoms. During this period she implemented several unpopular policies, including large-scale sterilization as a form of birth control. When long-postponed national elections were held in 1977, Gandhi and her party were defeated, and she left office. The Janata Party took over the government.

Early in 1978, Gandhi's supporters split from the Congress Party and formed the Congress (I) Party—the "I" signifying Indira. She was briefly imprisoned (October 1977 and December 1978) on charges of official corruption. Despite these setbacks, she won a new seat in

FROM THE MID-1900S TO THE LATE 1900S
LUCILLE BALL TO DIANA, PRINCESS OF WALES

During her four terms as India's prime minister, Indira Gandhi faced challenges from outside the country and inside her own party.

Parliament in November 1978, and her Congress (I) Party began to gather strength. Dissension within the ruling Janata Party led to the fall of its government in August 1979. When new elections for the Lok Sabha (lower house of Parliament) were held in January 1980, Gandhi and her Congress (I) Party were swept back into power in a landslide victory. Her son Sanjay Gandhi, who had become her chief political adviser, also won a seat in the Lok Sabha. All legal cases against Indira, and her son, were withdrawn.

Sanjay Gandhi's death in an airplane crash in June 1980 eliminated Indira's chosen successor from the political leadership of India. After Sanjay's death, she groomed her other son, Rajiv, for the leadership of her party. Indira Gandhi adhered to the quasi-socialist policies of industrial development that had been begun by her father. She established closer relations with the Soviet Union, depending on that nation for support in India's long-standing conflict with Pakistan.

During the early 1980s Gandhi was faced with threats to the political integrity of India. Several states sought a larger measure of independence from the central government, and Sikh separatists in Punjab state used violence to assert their demands for an autonomous state. In response, Gandhi ordered an army attack in June 1984 on the Harimandir (Golden Temple) at Amritsar, the Sikhs' holiest shrine, which led to the deaths of more than 450 Sikhs. Five months later, Gandhi was killed in her garden by bullets fired by two of her own Sikh bodyguards in revenge for the attack on the Golden Temple.

EVA PERÓN

(b. May 7, 1919, Los Toldos, Arg. — d. July 26, 1952, Buenos Aires)

Eva Duarte de Perón was the second wife of Argentine president Juan Perón. During her husband's first term as president (1946–52), she became a powerful though unofficial political leader, revered by the lower economic classes, who knew her as Evita.

Eva Duarte (in full María Eva Duarte) married Col. Juan Perón, a widower, in 1945 after an undistinguished career as a stage and radio actress. She participated in her husband's 1945–46 presidential campaign, winning the adulation of the masses, whom she addressed as *los descamisados* (Spanish: "the shirtless ones").

Although she never held any government post, Evita acted as de facto minister of health and labor, awarding generous wage increases to the unions, who responded with political support for Perón. After cutting off government subsidies to the traditional Sociedad de Beneficencia (Spanish: "Aid Society"), thereby making more enemies among the traditional elite, she replaced it with her own Eva Perón Foundation, which was supported by "voluntary" union and business contributions plus a substantial cut of the national lottery and other funds. These resources were used to establish thousands of hospitals, schools, orphanages, homes for the aged, and other charitable institutions. Evita was largely responsible for the passage of the women's suffrage law and formed the Peronista Feminist Party in 1949. She also introduced compulsory religious education into all Argentine schools. In 1951, although dying of cancer, she obtained the nomination for vice president, but the army forced her to withdraw her candidacy.

After her death, Evita remained a formidable influence in Argentine politics. Her working-class followers tried unsuccessfully to have her canonized, and her enemies, in an effort to exorcise her as a national symbol of Peronism, stole her embalmed body in 1955 after Juan Perón was overthrown and secreted it in Italy for 16 years. In 1971, the military government, bowing to Peronist demands, turned over her remains to her exiled widower in Madrid. After Juan Perón died in office in 1974, his third wife, Isabel Perón, hoping to gain favor among the populace, repatriated the remains and installed them next to the deceased leader in a crypt in the presidential palace. Two years later, a new military junta hostile to Peronism removed the bodies; Evita's remains were finally interred in the Duarte family crypt in Recoleta cemetery.

ROSALIND FRANKLIN
(b. July 25, 1920, London, Eng.—d. April 16, 1958, London)

The British scientist Rosalind Franklin was an unacknowledged contributor to the discovery of the molecular structure of deoxyribonucleic acid (DNA), a constituent of chromosomes that serves to encode genetic information.

Rosalind Elsie Franklin attended Saint Paul's Girls' School before studying physical chemistry at Newnham College, Cambridge. After graduating in 1941, she received a fellowship to conduct research in physical chemistry at Cambridge. But the advance of World War II changed her course of action: not only did she serve as a London air raid warden, but in 1942 she gave up her fellowship in order to work for the British Coal Utilisation Research Association, where she investigated the physical chemistry of carbon and coal for the war effort. Nevertheless, she was able to use this research for her doctoral thesis, and in 1945 she received a doctorate from Cambridge. From 1947 to 1950 she worked with Jacques Méring at the State Chemical Laboratory in Paris, studying X-ray diffraction technology. That work led to her research on the structural changes caused by the formation of graphite in heated carbons—work that was valuable for the coking industry.

In 1951, Franklin joined the Biophysical Laboratory at King's College, London, as a research fellow. There she applied X-ray diffraction methods to the study of DNA.

When she began her research at King's College, very little was known about the chemical makeup or structure of DNA. However, she soon discovered the density of DNA and, more important, established that the molecule existed in a helical conformation. Her work to make clearer X-ray patterns of DNA molecules laid the foundation for James Watson and Francis Crick to suggest in 1953 that the structure of DNA is a double-helix polymer, a spiral of two DNA strands wound around each other.

From 1953 to 1958 Franklin worked in the Crystallography Laboratory at Birkbeck College, London. While there she completed her work on coals and on DNA and began a project on the molecular structure of the tobacco mosaic virus. She collaborated on studies showing that the ribonucleic acid (RNA) in that virus was embedded in its protein rather than in its central cavity and that this RNA was a single-strand helix, rather than the double helix found in the DNA of bacterial viruses and higher organisms. Franklin's involvement in cutting-edge DNA research was halted by her untimely death from cancer in 1958.

ROSALYN S. YALOW

(b. July 19, 1921, New York, N.Y., U.S. — d. May 30, 2011, New York)

The American medical physicist Rosalyn Sussman Yalow was a joint recipient (with Andrew V. Schally and Roger Guillemin) of the 1977 Nobel Prize for Physiology or Medicine, awarded for her development of the radioimmunoassay (RIA), an extremely sensitive technique for measuring minute quantities of biologically active substances.

Yalow graduated with honors from Hunter College of the City University of New York in 1941 and four years later received her PhD in physics from the University of Illinois. From 1946 to 1950, she lectured on physics at

Hunter, and in 1947 she became a consultant in nuclear physics to the Bronx Veterans Administration Hospital, where from 1950 to 1970 she was physicist and assistant chief of the radioisotope service.

With a colleague, the American physician Solomon A. Berson, Yalow began using radioactive isotopes to examine and diagnose various disease conditions. Yalow and Berson's investigations into the mechanism underlying type II diabetes led to their development of RIA. In the 1950s, it was known that individuals treated with injections of animal insulin developed resistance to the hormone and so required greater amounts of it to offset the effects of the disease; however, a satisfactory explanation for this phenomenon had not been put forth. Yalow and Berson theorized that the foreign insulin stimulated the production of antibodies, which became bound to the insulin and prevented the hormone from entering cells and carrying out its function of metabolizing glucose. In order to prove their hypothesis to a skeptical scientific community, the researchers combined techniques from immunology and radioisotope tracing to measure minute amounts of these antibodies, and the RIA was born. It was soon apparent that this method could be used to measure hundreds of other biologically active substances, such as viruses, drugs, and other proteins. This made possible such practical applications as the screening of blood in blood banks for hepatitis virus and the determination of effective dosage levels of drugs and antibiotics.

In 1970, Yalow was appointed chief of the laboratory later renamed the Nuclear Medical Service at the Veterans Administration Hospital. In 1976, she was the first female recipient of the Albert Lasker Basic Medical Research Award. Yalow became a distinguished professor at large at the Albert Einstein College of Medicine at Yeshiva

University in 1979 and left in 1985 to accept the position of Solomon A. Berson Distinguished Professor at Large at the Mount Sinai School of Medicine. She was awarded the National Medal of Science in 1988.

NADINE GORDIMER

(b. Nov. 20, 1923, Springs, S.Af.—d. July 13, 2014, Johannesburg)

The South African novelist and short-story writer Nadine Gordimer examined the theme of exile and alienation in her works; she received the Nobel Prize for Literature in 1991.

Gordimer was born into a privileged white middle-class family and began reading at an early age. By the age of 9 she was writing, and she published her first story in a magazine when she was 15. Her wide reading informed her about the world on the other side of apartheid—the official South African policy of racial segregation—and that discovery in time developed into strong political opposition to apartheid. Never an outstanding scholar, she attended the University of Witwatersrand for one year. In addition to writing, she lectured and taught at various schools in the United States during the 1960s and '70s.

Gordimer's first book was *The Soft Voice of the Serpent* (1952), a collection of short stories. In 1953, a novel, *The Lying Days*, was published. Both exhibit the clear, controlled, and unsentimental technique that became her hallmark. Her stories concern the devastating effects of apartheid on South Africans—the constant tension between personal isolation and the commitment to social justice, the numbness caused by the unwillingness to accept apartheid, the inability to change it, and the refusal of exile.

In 1974 Gordimer won the Booker Prize for *The Conservationist* (1974). Later novels include *Burger's*

Daughter (1979), *July's People* (1981), *A Sport of Nature* (1987), and *My Son's Story* (1990). Gordimer addressed environmental issues in *Get a Life* (2005), the story of a South African ecologist who, after receiving thyroid treatment, becomes radioactive to others.

Gordimer wrote a number of short-story collections, including *A Soldier's Embrace* (1980), *Crimes of Conscience* (1991), and *Loot and Other Stories* (2003). *Living in Hope and History: Notes from Our Century* (1999) is a collection of essays, correspondence, and reminiscences. In 2007, Gordimer was awarded the French Legion of Honor.

ELIZABETH II

(b. April 21, 1926, London, Eng.—d. Sept. 8, 2022, Balmoral, Scot.)

Elizabeth II reigned as the queen of the United Kingdom of Great Britain and Northern Ireland from February 6, 1952, to September 8, 2022.

Elizabeth II, born Elizabeth Alexandra Mary, was the elder daughter of Albert, duke of York, and his wife, Lady Elizabeth Bowes-Lyon. As the child of a younger son of King George V, the young Elizabeth had little prospect of acceding to the throne until her uncle, Edward VIII (afterward duke of Windsor), abdicated in her father's favor on December 11, 1936, at which time her father became King George VI and she became heir presumptive. The princess's education was supervised by her mother, who entrusted her daughters to a governess, Marion Crawford; the princess was also grounded in history by C.H.K. Marten, afterward provost of Eton College, and had instruction from visiting teachers in music and languages. During World War II, she and her sister, Princess Margaret Rose, perforce spent much of their time safely away from the London blitz and separated from their parents, living mostly at Balmoral Castle in Scotland and at the Royal Lodge and Windsor Castle.

Early in 1947, Princess Elizabeth went with the king and queen to South Africa. After her return, there was an announcement of her betrothal to her distant cousin Lieutenant Philip Mountbatten of the Royal Navy, formerly Prince Philip of Greece and Denmark. The marriage took place in Westminster Abbey on November 20, 1947. On the eve of the wedding, her father, the king, conferred upon the bridegroom the titles of duke of Edinburgh, earl of Merioneth, and Baron Greenwich. They took residence at Clarence House in London. Their first child, Prince Charles (Charles Philip Arthur George), was born November 14, 1948, at Buckingham Palace.

In the summer of 1951, the health of King George VI entered into a serious decline, and Princess Elizabeth represented him at various state occasions. On October 7, she and her husband set out on a highly successful tour of Canada and Washington, DC. After Christmas in England, she and the duke set out in January 1952 for a tour of Australia and New Zealand, but en route, at Sagana, Kenya, news reached them of the king's death on February 6, 1952. Elizabeth, now queen, at once flew back to England. The first three months of her reign, the period of full mourning for her father, were passed in comparative seclusion. But in the summer, after she had moved from Clarence House to Buckingham Palace, she undertook the routine duties of the sovereign and carried out her first state opening of Parliament on November 4, 1952. Her coronation was held at Westminster Abbey on June 2, 1953.

Beginning in November 1953, the queen and the duke of Edinburgh made a six-month round-the-world tour of the Commonwealth, which included the first visit to Australia and New Zealand by a reigning British monarch. In 1957, after state visits to various European nations, she and the duke visited Canada and the United States. In 1961, she made the first royal British tour of the Indian subcontinent in 50 years, and she was also the first reigning British monarch to visit South America (in 1968) and the Persian Gulf countries (in 1979). During her "Silver Jubilee" in 1977, she presided at a London banquet attended by leaders of the 36 members of the Commonwealth, traveled Britain and Northern Ireland, and toured in the South Pacific and Australia, in Canada, and in the Caribbean.

On the accession of Queen Elizabeth, her son Prince Charles became heir apparent; he was named prince of Wales on July 26, 1958, and was so invested on July 1, 1969. The queen's other children were Princess Anne (Anne Elizabeth Alice Louise), born August 15, 1950; Prince Andrew (Andrew Albert Christian Edward), born February 19, 1960, and created duke of York in 1986; and Prince Edward (Edward Anthony Richard Louis), born March 10, 1964. All these children have the surname "of Windsor," but in 1960 Elizabeth decided to create the hyphenated name Mountbatten-Windsor for other descendants not styled prince or princess and royal highness. Elizabeth's first grandchild (Princess Anne's son) was born on November 15, 1977.

The queen seemed increasingly aware of the modern role of the monarchy, allowing, for example, the televising of the royal family's domestic life in 1970 and condoning the formal dissolution of her sister's marriage in 1978. However, after the failed marriage of her son and Diana, princess of Wales, and Diana's death in 1997, popular feeling in Britain turned against the royal family, which was thought to be out of touch with contemporary British life. In line with her earlier attempts at modernizing the monarchy, the queen, after 1997, sought to present a less-stuffy and less-traditional image of the monarchy. These attempts met with mixed success.

In August 2017, Prince Philip officially retired from public life. In the meantime, Elizabeth began to reduce her own official engagements. Philip, Elizabeth's husband of more than seven decades, died in April 2021.

In June 2022, Britain celebrated Elizabeth's 70 years on the throne with the "Platinum Jubilee," a four-day national holiday. On September 8, 2022, Elizabeth's death, at age 96, shocked Britain and the world. Prince Charles succeeded her on the throne as King Charles III. Ten days of national commemoration of her life and legacy followed.

Queen Elizabeth was known to favor simplicity in court life and take a serious and informed interest in government business, aside from the traditional and ceremonial duties. Privately, she became a keen horsewoman. Her financial and property holdings made her one of the world's richest women.

ANNE FRANK

(b. June 12, 1929, Frankfurt am Main, Ger.—d. March 1945, Bergen-Belsen concentration camp, near Hannover)

Anne Frank, a young Jewish girl who wrote a diary of her family's two years in hiding during the German occupation of The Netherlands, personalized the Holocaust for generations of readers. *The Diary of a Young Girl* (published after her death) has become a classic of war literature.

Early in the Nazi regime of Adolf Hitler, Anne's father, Otto Frank (1889–1980), a German businessman, took his wife and two daughters to live in Amsterdam. In 1941, after German forces occupied The Netherlands, Anne was compelled to transfer from a public to a Jewish school. Faced with deportation (supposedly to a forced-labor camp), the Franks went into hiding on July 9, 1942, with four other Jews in the back-room office and warehouse of Otto Frank's food-products business. With the aid of a few non-Jewish friends who smuggled in food and other supplies, they lived confined to their secret annex until August 4, 1944, when the Gestapo, acting on a tip from Dutch informers, discovered them.

The family was transported to Westerbork, a transit camp in The Netherlands, and from there to Auschwitz in German-occupied Poland on September 3, 1944, on the last transport to leave Westerbork for Auschwitz. Anne (in full Annelies Marie) and her sister Margot were transferred to Bergen-Belsen the following month. Anne's mother died in early January, just before the evacuation of Auschwitz on January 18, 1945. Both Anne and Margot died in a typhus epidemic in March 1945, only weeks before the liberation of Bergen-Belsen. Otto Frank was found hospitalized at Auschwitz when it was liberated by Russian troops on January 27, 1945.

Friends who had searched the family's hiding place after their capture later gave Otto Frank the papers left behind by the Gestapo. Among them he found Anne's diary, which was published as *The Diary of a Young Girl* (originally in Dutch, 1947). Precocious in style and insight, it traces her emotional growth amid adversity. In it she wrote, "In spite of everything I still believe that people are really good at heart."

The diary has been translated into more than 65 languages and is the most widely read diary of the Holocaust, and Anne is probably the best-known Holocaust victim. A new English translation, published in 1995, contained material edited out of the original version, making the new work nearly one-third longer. The Frank family's hiding place on the Prinsengracht—a canal in Amsterdam—has become a museum.

FROM THE MID-1900S TO THE LATE 1900S
LUCILLE BALL TO DIANA, PRINCESS OF WALES

Anne Frank's writings, which were published after her death, still have the power to touch people today.

VIOLETA BARRIOS DE CHAMORRO
(b. Oct. 18, 1929, Rivas, Nic.)

Newspaper publisher and politician Violeta Barrios de Chamorro was Central America's first woman president and served as leader of Nicaragua from 1990 to 1997.

Violeta Barrios was born into a wealthy Nicaraguan family (her father was a cattle rancher). She received much of her early education in the U.S. states of Texas and Virginia. In 1950, shortly after the death of her father, she returned to Nicaragua, where she married Pedro Joaquim Chamorro Cardenal, editor of the newspaper *La Prensa*, which was often critical of the Somoza family dictatorship. The Chamorros were forced into exile in 1957 and lived in Costa Rica for several years before returning to Nicaragua after the Somoza government declared an amnesty.

On January 10, 1978, Pedro Chamorro, who had continued to criticize the Somozas and had been imprisoned several times during the 1960s and '70s, was assassinated. His death helped to spark a revolution, led by the Sandinista National Liberation Front, which toppled the government of Anastasio Somoza Debayle in July 1979. A member of the Sandinista ruling junta in 1979–80, Violeta Chamorro soon became disillusioned with the Sandinistas' Marxist policies, and later she became an outspoken foe. She took over *La Prensa*, which was frequently shut down during the 1980s and was banned completely for a period in 1986–87. During the 1980s she was accused by the Sandinistas of accepting money from the U.S. Central Intelligence Agency, which was then providing support to opposition groups and directing the Contra rebels in their guerrilla war against the Sandinista government.

An end to the guerrilla war was negotiated in the late 1980s, and free elections were scheduled for 1990.

Chamorro, drafted as the presidential candidate of the 14-party National Opposition Union (Unión Nacional Opositor; UNO) alliance, won a surprisingly easy victory over President Daniel Ortega Saavedra, head of the Sandinistas. She was inaugurated on April 25, 1990, becoming Central America's first woman president.

During her presidency Chamorro reversed a number of Sandinista policies. Several state-owned industries were privatized, censorship was lifted, and the size of the army was reduced. At the same time, she retained a number of Sandinistas in the government and attempted to reconcile the country's various political factions. Many credit her conciliatory policies with helping to maintain the fragile peace that had been negotiated. Barred from running for a second term, she retired from politics after her term ended in January 1997.

SANDRA DAY O'CONNOR

(b. March 26, 1930, El Paso, Texas, U.S.)

Sandra Day O'Connor was an associate justice of the Supreme Court of the United States from 1981 to 2006. She was the first woman to serve on the Supreme Court. A moderate conservative, she was known for her dispassionate and meticulously researched opinions.

O'Connor grew up on a large family ranch near Duncan, Arizona. She received undergraduate (1950) and law (1952) degrees from Stanford University, where she met the future chief justice of the United States William Rehnquist. Upon her graduation, she married a classmate, John Jay O'Connor III. Unable to find employment in a law firm because she was a woman—despite her academic achievements, one firm offered her a job as a secretary—she became a deputy district attorney in San Mateo county,

California. After a brief tenure, she and her husband, a member of the U.S. Army Judge Advocate General Corps, moved to Germany, where she served as a civil attorney for the army (1954–57).

Upon her return to the United States, O'Connor pursued private practice in Maryville, Arizona, becoming an assistant attorney general for the state (1965–69). In 1969, she was elected as a Republican to the Arizona Senate (1969–74), rising to the position of majority leader—the first woman in the United States to occupy such a position. In 1974, she was elected a Superior Court judge in Maricopa county, and in 1979 she was appointed to the Arizona Court of Appeals in Phoenix. In July 1981, President Ronald Reagan nominated her to fill the vacancy left on the Supreme Court by the retirement of Justice Potter Stewart. Described by Reagan as a "person for all seasons," O'Connor was confirmed unanimously by the Senate and was sworn in as the first female justice on September 25, 1981.

O'Connor quickly became known for her pragmatism and was considered, with Justice Anthony Kennedy, a decisive swing vote in the Supreme Court's decisions. In such disparate fields as election law and abortion rights, she attempted to fashion workable solutions to major constitutional questions, often over the course of several cases. In her decisions in election law, she emphasized the importance of equal-protection claims (*Shaw v. Reno*, [1993]), declared unconstitutional district boundaries that are "unexplainable on grounds other than race" (*Bush v. Vera*, [1996]), and sided with the court's more liberal members in upholding the configuration of a congressional district in North Carolina that was created on the basis of variables including but not limited to race (*Easley v. Cromartie*, [2001]).

In similar fashion, O'Connor's views on abortion rights were articulated gradually. In a series of rulings, she signaled a reluctance to support any decision that would deny women the right to choose a safe and legal abortion. By "defecting" in part from the conservative majority in *Webster v. Reproductive Health Services* (1989)—in which the court upheld a Missouri law that prohibited public employees from performing or assisting in abortions not necessary to save a woman's life and that required doctors to determine the viability of a fetus if it was at least 20 weeks old—she reduced the court's opinion to a plurality. Through her stewardship in *Planned Parenthood of Southeastern Pennsylvania v. Casey* (1992), the court refashioned its position on the right to abortion. The court's opinion, which O'Connor wrote with Justices Anthony Kennedy and David Souter, reaffirmed the constitutionally protected right to abortion established in *Roe v. Wade* (1973) but also lowered the standard that legal restrictions on abortion must meet in order to pass constitutional muster. After *Casey*, such laws would be considered unconstitutional only if they constituted an "undue burden" on women seeking to obtain an abortion.

In 2006, O'Connor retired from the Supreme Court and was replaced by Samuel Alito. In 2009, she was awarded the Presidential Medal of Freedom.

ELLEN JOHNSON SIRLEAF
(b. Oct. 29, 1938, Monrovia, Liberia)

The Liberian politician and economist Ellen Johnson Sirleaf was president of Liberia from 2006 to 2018. She was the first woman to be elected head of state of an African country. Johnson Sirleaf was one of three recipients of the 2011 Nobel Prize for Peace for her efforts to further women's rights.

Of mixed Gola and German heritage, Ellen Johnson was the daughter of the first indigenous Liberian to sit in the national legislature. At age 17, she married James Sirleaf (they were later divorced). In 1961, Johnson Sirleaf went to the United States to study economics and business administration. After obtaining a master's degree (1971) in public administration from Harvard University, she entered government service in Liberia.

She served as assistant minister of finance (1972–73) under President William Tolbert and as finance minister (1980–85) in Samuel K. Doe's military dictatorship. Johnson Sirleaf became known for her personal financial integrity and clashed with both heads of state.

During Doe's regime, she was imprisoned twice and narrowly avoided execution. In the 1985 national election, she campaigned for a seat in the Senate and openly criticized the military government, which led to her arrest and a 10-year prison sentence. She was released after a short time and allowed to leave the country. During 12 years of exile in Kenya and the United States, she became an influential economist for the World Bank, Citibank, and other international financial institutions. From 1992 to 1997, she was the director of the Regional Bureau for Africa of the United Nations Development Programme.

Johnson Sirleaf ran for president in the 1997 election, representing the Unity Party. She finished second to Charles Taylor and was forced back into exile when his government charged her with treason. By 1999, Liberia had collapsed into civil war. After Taylor went into exile in 2003, Johnson Sirleaf returned to Liberia to chair the Commission on Good Governance, which oversaw preparations for democratic elections. In 2005, she again ran for president, vowing to end civil strife and corruption, establish unity, and rebuild the country's devastated infrastructure. Known as the "Iron Lady," she placed second in the first round of voting, and on November 8, 2005, she won the runoff election, defeating football (soccer) legend George Weah. Johnson Sirleaf was sworn in as president of Liberia on January 16, 2006.

With more than 15,000 United Nations peacekeepers in the country and unemployment running at 80 percent, Johnson Sirleaf faced serious challenges. She immediately sought debt amelioration and aid from the international community. In addition, she established a Truth and Reconciliation Committee to probe corruption and heal ethnic tensions.

Economic progress continued during Johnson Sirleaf's second term, begun in 2011, until the country was hit with the devastating Ebola virus disease in 2014. Over the course of the next two years, the disease killed more than 4,800 Liberians, crippled the country's economy, and erased many of the country's hard-fought gains of the previous postwar decade.

On January 22, 2018, Johnson Sirleaf stepped down as president. It was the first transfer of power between democratically elected leaders in Liberia since 1944.

GRO HARLEM BRUNDTLAND
(b. April 20, 1939, Oslo, Nor.)

Having served three terms as prime minister of Norway in the 1980s and '90s, Gro Harlem Brundtland later was director general of the World Health Organization (WHO; 1998–2003). Trained as a physician, she became identified with public health and environmental issues and with the rights of women.

The daughter of a physician and politician, she received an MD degree from the University of Oslo in 1963 and a master's degree in public health from Harvard University in 1965. She then worked as a public health officer for the city of Oslo and for Oslo schools. A member of the Labor Party, she was minister of the environment from 1974 to 1979, and she was first elected to the Storting (parliament) in 1977. In 1975, she was elected deputy leader of the party and in 1981 its leader.

When the Labor prime minister resigned in 1981, Brundtland was appointed to the post, the youngest person and first woman to become prime minister of Norway. She served for only nine months, because Labor lost the elections held later that year. She returned as prime minister in 1986–89 and served again in 1990–96 until her resignation. Brundtland never had fewer than 8 women in her 18-member cabinet and, overall, is credited with securing better educational and economic opportunities for women in Norway. In 1983, she became chair of the UN World Commission on Environment and Development, which in 1987 issued *Our Common Future*, the report that introduced the idea of "sustainable development" and led to the first Earth Summit. In 1998, she became director general of the WHO, where she tackled global pandemics such as AIDS and SARS; her term ended in 2003. In 2007, together with Han Seung-soo, former minister of foreign affairs of South Korea, and Ricardo Lagos Escobar, a former president of Chile, she was appointed a special envoy on climate change to Ban Ki-moon, the secretary-general of the United Nations. She held the post until 2010.

WANGARI MAATHAI

(b. April 1, 1940, Nyeri, Kenya—d. Sept. 25, 2011, Nairobi)

In 2004, the Kenyan politician and environmental activist Wangari Muta Maathai was awarded the Nobel Prize for Peace, becoming the first Black African woman to win the award. Her work often has been considered both unwelcome and subversive in her own country, where her outspokenness has constituted stepping far outside traditional gender roles.

Maathai was educated in the United States at Mount Saint Scholastica College (now Benedictine College; BS in biology, 1964) and at the University of Pittsburgh (MS, 1966). In 1971, she received a PhD at the University of Nairobi, effectively becoming the first woman in either East or Central Africa to earn a doctorate. She began teaching in the Department of Veterinary Anatomy at the University of Nairobi after graduation, and in 1977 she became chair of the department.

While working with the National Council of Women of Kenya, Maathai developed the idea that village women could improve the environment by planting trees to provide a fuel source and to slow the processes of deforestation and desertification. The Green Belt Movement, an organization she founded in 1977, had by the early 21st century planted some 30 million trees. Leaders of the Green Belt Movement established the Pan African Green Belt Network in 1986 in order to educate world leaders about conservation and environmental improvement. As a result of the movement's activism, similar initiatives were begun in other African countries, including Tanzania, Ethiopia, and Zimbabwe.

In addition to her conservation work, Maathai was also an advocate for human rights, AIDS prevention, and women's issues, and she frequently represented these concerns at meetings of the United Nations General Assembly. She was elected to Kenya's National Assembly in 2002 with 98 percent of the vote, and in 2003 she was appointed assistant minister of environment, natural resources, and wildlife. When she won the Nobel Prize in 2004, the committee commended her "holistic approach to sustainable development that embraces democracy, human rights, and women's rights in particular."

Her first book, *The Green Belt Movement: Sharing the Approach and the Experience* (1988; rev. ed. 2003), detailed the history of the organization. She published an autobiography, *Unbowed*, in 2007. Another volume, *The Challenge for Africa* (2009), criticized Africa's leadership as ineffectual and urged Africans to try to solve their problems without Western assistance.

MARTHA STEWART
(b. Aug. 3, 1941, Jersey City, N.J., U.S.)

Martha Stewart, an American entrepreneur and domestic lifestyle innovator, built a catering business into an international media and home furnishing corporation, Martha Stewart Living Omnimedia Inc.

Raised in Nutley, New Jersey, Martha Helen Kostyra grew up in a Polish American household where the traditional arts of cooking, sewing, canning and preserving, housekeeping, and gardening were practiced. She started planning birthday parties for neighbor children while she was in grammar school, and she paid her college tuition by taking modeling jobs in New York City. She married law student Andrew Stewart (1961; they divorced in 1990) while studying at Barnard College (BA, European history and architectural history, 1963); their daughter, Alexis, was born in 1965. Stewart worked as a stockbroker at a small Wall Street firm (1965–72) until she and her family moved to Westport, Connecticut, and turned their ambitions toward restoring Turkey Hill, a Federal-style farmhouse. With yeoman labor they gardened, restored, and decorated, acquiring the skills and the setting for books and TV shows.

After launching a catering business (1976) with a partner, Norma Collier, Stewart's talent for innovation and presentation attracted a string of prestigious clients. Her first book, *Entertaining* (1982; with Elizabeth Hawes), set the tone for subsequent publications: superb art direction, gorgeous settings, labor-intensive recipes and decorating projects. In addition, she oversaw the *CBS Masterworks Dinner Classics*, a series of music compilations that could provide the appropriate background music for a picnic, cocktail party, Sunday brunch, or exotic meal.

Following continued success with such books as *Martha Stewart's Hors d'Oeuvres* (1984) and *Weddings* (1987), Time Publishing Ventures Inc. teamed with Stewart (1990) to publish a monthly magazine, *Martha Stewart Living*, with Stewart not only as editor in chief but as the featured personality within its pages. She began a syndicated television show of the same name (1993) and eventually bought the magazine from Time Warner Inc. (1997), funding the purchase with proceeds from her merchandising arrangement with Kmart, which debuted as the Martha Stewart Everyday line of household furnishings. Each of these business moves took her closer to her ultimate goal of creating a multichannel media and marketing firm. That goal was fully realized when Martha Stewart Living Omnimedia was listed on the New York Stock Exchange (1999), with Stewart as chairman and chief executive officer (CEO). She became a billionaire, however briefly, with the public launch of her company.

In December 2001, Stewart ordered the sale of 4,000 shares of ImClone Systems, a biomedical firm owned by family friend Samuel Waksal. The sale of her shares, occurring one day before public information about ImClone caused the stock price to drop, sparked accusations of insider trading. Stewart stepped down as CEO of her firm in 2003, assuming the title of chief creative officer and appearing to distance herself from daily operations as she focused on defending herself against charges of lying and obstructing justice. Convicted in 2004 and sentenced to serve five months in prison followed by five months of home detention, Stewart urged her fans to continue supporting her company.

As she built her business, Stewart's perfectionism, comprehensive knowledge, and bottomless capacity for work were not universally admired. She was censured for setting an impossible model for harried working mothers, and her glorification of a home-centered existence seemed to some a step backward for women. But many criticisms were swept away by the personal appeal that made her company a commercial success.

CHRISTIANE NÜSSLEIN-VOLHARD
(b. Oct. 20, 1942, Magdeburg, Ger.)

The German developmental geneticist Christiane Nüsslein-Volhard was jointly awarded the 1995 Nobel Prize for Physiology or Medicine with geneticists Eric F. Wieschaus and Edward B. Lewis for their research concerning the mechanisms of early embryonic development. Nüsslein-Volhard, working in tandem with Wieschaus, expanded upon the pioneering work of Lewis, who used the fruit fly, or vinegar fly (*Drosophila melanogaster*), as a subject. Her work has relevance to the development of all multicellular organisms, including humans.

At Eberhard-Karl University of Tübingen, Nüsslein-Volhard received a diploma in biochemistry in 1968 and a doctorate in genetics in 1973. After holding fellowships in Basel and Freiburg, she joined Wieschaus as a group leader at the European Molecular Biology Laboratory in Heidelberg in 1978. In 1981, she returned to Tübingen, where, in 1985, she became director of the Max Planck Institute for Developmental Biology.

At Heidelberg, Nüsslein-Volhard and Wieschaus spent more than a year crossbreeding 40,000 fruit fly families and systematically examining their genetic makeup at a dual microscope. Their trial-and-error methods resulted in the discovery that of the fly's 20,000 genes, about 5,000 are deemed important to early development and about 140 are essential. They assigned responsibility for the fruit fly's embryonic development to three genetic categories: gap genes, which lay out the head-to-tail body plan; pair-rule genes, which determine body segmentation; and segment-polarity genes, which establish repeating structures within each segment.

In the early 1990s Nüsslein-Volhard began studying genes that control development in the zebra fish *Danio rerio*. These organisms are ideal models for investigations into developmental biology because they have clear embryos, have a rapid rate of reproduction, and are closely related to other vertebrates. Nüsslein-Volhard studied the migration of cells from their sites of origin to their sites of destination within zebra fish embryos. Her investigations in zebra fish have helped elucidate genes and other cellular substances involved in human development and in the regulation of normal human physiology.

In addition to the Nobel Prize, Nüsslein-Volhard received the Leibniz Prize (1986) and the Albert Lasker Basic Medical Research Award (1991). She also published several books, including *Zebrafish: A Practical Approach* (2002; written with Ralf Dahm) and *Coming to Life: How Genes Drive Development* (2006).

BILLIE JEAN KING
(b. Nov. 22, 1943, Long Beach, Calif., U.S.)

The American athlete and tennis player Billie Jean King (née Billie Jean Moffitt) is noteworthy for having elevated the status of women's professional tennis through her influence and playing style, beginning in the late 1960s. In her career, she won 39 major titles, competing in both singles and doubles.

King was athletically inclined from an early age. She first attracted international attention in 1961 by winning the Wimbledon doubles championship with Karen Hantz; theirs was the youngest team to win. She went on to capture a record 20 Wimbledon titles (singles 1966–68, 1972–73, and 1975; women's doubles 1961–62, 1965, 1967–68, 1970–73, 1979; mixed doubles 1967, 1971, 1973–74), in addition to U.S. singles (1967, 1971–72, 1974), French singles (1972), and the Australian title (1968); her Wimbledon record was tied by Martina Navratilova in 2003. She was perhaps one of the greatest doubles players in the history of tennis, winning 27 major titles. With her victories in 1967, she was the first woman since 1938 to sweep the U.S. and British singles, doubles, and mixed doubles titles in a single year.

King turned professional after 1968 and became the first woman athlete to win more than $100,000 in one season (1971). In 1973, she beat the aging Bobby Riggs in a much-publicized "Battle of the Sexes" match. The match set a record for the largest tennis audience and the largest purse awarded up to that time. She pushed relentlessly for the rights of women players, helped to form a separate women's tour, and obtained financial backing from commercial sponsors. She was one of the founders and the first president (1974) of the Women's Tennis Association.

King and her husband, Larry King (married 1965), were

From the Mid-1900s to the Late 1900s
Lucille Ball to Diana, Princess of Wales

In addition to winning many titles, Billie Jean King made women's tennis a sport distinct from the men's game and increased winners' purses on the women's tour.

part of a group that founded World Team Tennis (WTT) in 1974. King served as the player-coach of the Philadelphia Freedoms, thus becoming one of the first women to coach professional male athletes. The WTT folded after 1978 because of financial losses, but King revived the competition in 1981.

King retired from competitive tennis in 1984 and the same year became the first woman commissioner in professional sports in her position with the World Team Tennis League. She was inducted into the Women's Sports Hall of Fame in 1980, the International Tennis Hall of Fame in 1987, and the National Women's Hall of Fame in 1990. King remained active in tennis and since the mid-1990s served as coach for several Olympic and Federation Cup teams. The United States Tennis Association honored King in August 2006, when it renamed the National Tennis Center, home of the U.S. Open, the Billie Jean King National Tennis Center. She published two autobiographies, *Billie Jean* (1974; with Kim Chapin) and *The Autobiography of Billie Jean King* (1982; with Frank Deford), as well as *We Have Come a Long Way: The Story of Women's Tennis* (1988; with Cynthia Starr) and *Pressure Is a Privilege: Lessons I've Learned from Life and the Battle of the Sexes* (2008; with Christine Brennan).

MARY ROBINSON
(b. May 21, 1944, Ballina, County Mayo, Ire.)

The Irish lawyer, politician, and diplomat Mary Robinson served as president of Ireland (1990–97) and as United Nations High Commissioner for Human Rights (UNHCHR; 1997–2002).

Robinson, born Mary Teresa Winifred Bourke, was educated at Trinity College and King's Inns in Dublin and at Harvard University in the United States. She served at Trinity College (University of Dublin) as Reid Professor of penal legislation, constitutional and criminal law, and the law of evidence (1969–75) and lecturer in European Community law (1975–90). In 1988, she established (with her husband) at Trinity College the Irish Centre for European Law. A distinguished constitutional lawyer and a renowned supporter of human rights, she was elected to the Royal Irish Academy and was a member of the International Commission of Jurists in Geneva (1987–90). She sat in the Seanad (upper chamber of Parliament) for the Trinity College constituency (1969–89) and served as whip for the Labour Party until resigning from the party over the Anglo-Irish Agreement of 1985, which she felt ignored unionist objections. She was a member of the Dublin City Council (1979–83) and ran unsuccessfully in 1977 and 1981 for Dublin parliamentary constituencies.

Nominated by the Labour Party and supported by the Green Party and the Workers' Party, Robinson became Ireland's first woman president in 1990 by mobilizing a liberal constituency and merging it with a more conservative constituency opposed to the Fianna Fáil party. As president, Robinson adopted a much more prominent role than her predecessors, and she did much to communicate a more modern image of Ireland. Strongly committed to human rights, she was the first head of state to visit Somalia after it suffered from civil war and famine in 1992 and the first to visit Rwanda after the genocide in that country in 1994. Shortly before her term as president expired, she took up the post of UNHCHR. As high commissioner, Robinson changed the priorities of her office to emphasize the promotion of human rights at the national and regional levels; she was the first UNHCHR to visit China, and she also helped to improve the monitoring of human rights in Kosovo. In 2001, Robinson served as secretary-general of the World Conference against Racism, Racial Discrimination, Xenophobia and Related Intolerance, held in Durban, South Africa. In 1998, she was elected chancellor of Trinity College.

After leaving her post at the UN, Robinson founded the nongovernmental organization Realizing Rights: The Ethical Globalization Initiative, in 2002. Its central concerns included equitable international trade, access to health care, migration, women's leadership, and corporate responsibility. She was also a founding member of the Council of Women World Leaders, an honorary president of Oxfam International (an organization that provides relief and development aid to impoverished or disaster-stricken communities worldwide), and a member of the Club of Madrid (which promotes democracy). In 2004, she received the Amnesty International Ambassador of Conscience award for her human rights work.

AUNG SAN SUU KYI

(b. June 19, 1945, Rangoon, Burma [now Yangon, Myanmar])

The Myanmar opposition leader Aung San Suu Kyi is the daughter of Aung San (a martyred national hero of independent Burma) and Khin Kyi (a prominent Burmese diplomat), and winner in 1991 of the Nobel Prize for Peace. She held multiple governmental posts from 2016, including that of state counselor, which essentially made her the de facto leader of the country. She was sidelined in February 2021 when the military seized power.

Aung San Suu Kyi was 2 years old when her father, then the de facto prime minister of what would shortly become independent Burma, was assassinated. She attended schools in Burma until 1960, when her mother was appointed ambassador to India. After further study in

India, she attended the University of Oxford, where she met her future husband. She had two children and lived a rather quiet life until 1988, when she returned to Burma to nurse her dying mother. There the mass slaughter of protesters against the brutal and unresponsive rule of the military strongman U Ne Win led her to speak out and begin a nonviolent struggle for democracy and human rights.

In July 1989, the military government of the newly named Union of Myanmar placed Aung San Suu Kyi under house arrest and held her incommunicado. The military offered to free her if she agreed to leave Myanmar, but she refused to do so until the country was returned to civilian government and political prisoners were freed. The newly formed group she became affiliated with, the National League for Democracy (NLD), won more than 80 percent of the contested parliamentary seats in 1990, but the election results were ignored by the military government.

Aung San Suu Kyi was freed from house arrest in July 1995. The following year she attended the NLD party congress, but the military government continued to harass both her and her party. In 1998, she announced the formation of a representative committee that she declared was the country's legitimate ruling parliament. The military junta once again placed her under house arrest from September 2000 to May 2002. Following clashes between the NLD and pro-government demonstrators in 2003, the government returned her to house arrest. Calls for her release continued throughout the international community in the face of her sentence's annual renewal. In August 2009, she was convicted of breaching the terms of her house arrest and sentenced to an additional 18 months. The conviction was likely designed to prevent her from participating in elections scheduled for 2010. Suu Kyi was released from house arrest six days after the election.

In January 2012, Suu Kyi announced that she was seeking election to a constituency in Yangon. She easily won her seat and was sworn into office on May 2. On March 15, 2016, legislative members elected her close confidant, Htin Kyaw, to serve as the country's new president. He was inaugurated on March 30.

Suu Kyi was then named state counselor, a position newly created by the legislature and signed into law by Htin Kyaw; the post was similar to that of prime minister and potentially more powerful than the president. The creation of the state counselor role for Suu Kyi rankled the military, whose legislative members denounced the bill that provided for the new position as being unconstitutional and refused to take part in the vote on the bill.

In her new role, Suu Kyi focused on finding peace with the country's many ethnic armed organizations, of which 20 or so were engaged in active insurgencies. She and her administration faced widespread international condemnation over the treatment of the Muslim Rohingya people of Myanmar's Rakhine state. After some attacks by Rohingya militants on security installations in 2016 and 2017, the military and police embarked on a brutal campaign against the entire group, allegedly committing human rights abuses and causing a large percentage of the population to flee the country. Given Suu Kyi's history as a champion of human rights and democracy, sharp criticism was directed at her for initially seeming to ignore the crisis and, when she did address it, not denouncing the actions of the security forces or intervening. In protest of her inaction regarding the Rohingya, several organizations revoked her human rights-related honors and awards.

Although Suu Kyi's reputation had suffered abroad, at home she and the NLD still retained a good amount of support. In the November 8, 2020, parliamentary elections, the NLD won a commanding majority of seats in both legislative chambers and was poised to form the next government. The military and its aligned party decried the results as being fraudulent and appealed to the electoral commission, which dismissed their claims.

The newly elected parliament was due to hold its first session on February 1, 2021, but, in the early hours of that day, the military seized power in a coup d'etat. Suu Kyi and other NLD leaders were detained by the military and later tried. Meanwhile, work strikes and other acts of civil disobedience ensued in the weeks following the coup, as did large-scale protests calling for her release.

SHIRIN EBADI
(b. June 21, 1947, Hamadan, Iran)

For her efforts to promote democracy and human rights, especially those of women and children in Iran, Shirin Ebadi received the Nobel Prize for Peace in 2003. She was the first Muslim woman and the first Iranian to receive the award.

Ebadi was born into an educated Iranian family; her father was an author and a lecturer in commercial law. When she was an infant, her family moved to Tehrān. Ebadi attended Anoshiravn Dadgar and Reza Shah Kabir schools before earning a law degree, in only three and a half years, from the University of Tehrān (1969). That same year she took an apprenticeship at the Department of Justice and became one of the first women judges in Iran. While serving as a judge, she also earned a doctorate in private law from the University of Tehrān (1971). From 1975 to 1979 she was head of the city court of Tehrān.

After the 1979 revolution and the establishment of an Islamic republic, women were deemed unsuitable to serve as judges because the new leaders believed that Islam forbids it. Ebadi was subsequently forced to become a clerk of the court. After she and other female judges protested this action, they were given higher roles within the Department of Justice but were still not allowed to serve as judges. Ebadi resigned in protest. She then chose to practice law but was initially denied a lawyer's license. In 1992, after years of struggle, she finally obtained a license to practice law and began to do so. She also taught at the University of Tehrān and became an advocate for civil rights.

In court Ebadi defended women and dissidents and represented many people who, like her, had run afoul of the Iranian government. She also distributed evidence implicating government officials in the 1999 murders of students at the University of Tehrān, for which she was jailed for three weeks in 2000. Found guilty of "disturbing public opinion," she was given a prison term, barred from practicing law for five years, and fined, although her sentence was later suspended.

Ebadi helped found the Defenders of Human Rights Center, but it was closed by the government in 2008. Later that year her law offices were raided, and in 2009 Ebadi went into exile in the United Kingdom. However, she continued to agitate for reforms in Iran.

Ebadi wrote a number of books on the subject of human rights. These include *The Rights of the Child: A Study of Legal Aspects of Children's Rights in Iran* (1994), *History and Documentation of Human Rights in Iran* (2000), and *The Rights of Women* (2002). She also was founder and head of the Association for Support of Children's Rights in Iran. In addition to writing books on human rights, Ebadi reflected on her own experiences in *Iran Awakening: From Prison to Peace Prize, One Woman's Struggle at the Crossroads* (2006; with Azadeh Moaveni).

HILLARY RODHAM CLINTON
(b. Oct. 26, 1947, Chicago, Ill., U.S.)

The American lawyer and politician Hillary Rodham Clinton served as a U.S. senator (2001–09) and secretary of state (2009– 2013) in the administration of President Barack Obama. She also served as first lady (1993–2001) during the administration of her husband, Bill Clinton, 42nd president of the United States. As the Democratic Party's nominee for president in 2016, she became the first woman to top the presidential ticket of a major party in the United States.

Hillary Diane Rodham was the eldest child of Hugh and Dorothy Rodham. She grew up in Park Ridge, Illinois, where her father's textile business provided the family with a comfortable income. Her parents' emphasis on hard work and academic excellence set high standards.

A student leader in public schools, she was active in youth programs at the First United Methodist Church. Although she later became associated with liberal causes, during this time she adhered to the Republican Party of her parents. She campaigned for Republican presidential candidate Barry Goldwater in 1964 and chaired the local chapter of the Young Republicans. A year later, after she enrolled at Wellesley College, her political views began to change. Influenced by the assassinations of Malcolm X, Robert F. Kennedy, and Martin Luther King Jr., she joined the Democratic Party and volunteered in the presidential campaign of antiwar candidate Eugene McCarthy.

After her graduation from Wellesley in 1969, Clinton entered Yale Law School, where she came under the influence of Yale alumna Marian Wright Edelman, a lawyer and children's rights advocate. Through her work with Edelman, she developed a strong interest in family law and issues affecting children.

Although Hillary met Bill Clinton at Yale, they took separate paths after graduation in 1973. He returned to his native Arkansas, and she worked with Edelman in Massachusetts for the Children's Defense Fund. In 1974, Hillary participated in the Watergate inquiry into the possible impeachment of President Richard M. Nixon. When her assignment ended with Nixon's resignation in August 1974, she moved to Arkansas. She taught at the University of Arkansas School of Law, and, following her marriage to Bill Clinton on October 11, 1975, she joined the prominent Rose Law Firm in Little Rock, Arkansas, where she later became a partner.

After Bill was elected governor of Arkansas in 1978, she continued to pursue her career and retained her maiden name (until 1982), bringing considerable criticism from voters who felt that her failure to change her name indicated a lack of commitment to her husband. Their only child, Chelsea Victoria, was born in 1980.

Throughout Bill's tenure as governor (1979–81, 1983–92), Hillary worked on programs that aided children and the disadvantaged; she also maintained a successful law practice. She served on the boards of several high-profile corporations and was twice named one of the nation's 100 most influential lawyers (1988, 1991) by the *National Law Journal*. She also served as chair of the Arkansas Education Standards Committee and founded the Arkansas Advocates for Children and Families.

In Bill's 1992 presidential campaign, Hillary played a crucial role by greeting voters, giving speeches, and serving as one of her husband's chief advisers. Her appearance with him on the television news program *60 Minutes* in January 1992 made her name a household word. Responding to questions about Bill's alleged 12-year sexual relationship with an Arkansas woman, Gennifer Flowers, Bill and Hillary discussed their marital problems, and Hillary told voters to judge her husband by his record—adding that, if they did not like what they saw, then, "heck, don't vote for him."

With a professional career unequaled by any previous presidential candidate's wife, Hillary was heavily scrutinized. Conservatives complained that she had her own agenda, because she had worked for some liberal causes. During one campaign stop, she defended herself from such criticism by asserting that she could have "stayed home and baked cookies." This impromptu remark was used by her critics as evidence of her lack of respect for women who are full-time homemakers.

Some of Hillary's financial dealings raised suspicions of impropriety and led to major investigations after she became first lady. Her investment in Whitewater, a real estate development in Arkansas, and her commodities trading in 1978–79—through which she reportedly turned a $1,000 investment into $100,000 in a few months—came under close scrutiny.

During the 1992 campaign, Bill Clinton sometimes spoke of a "twofer" ("two for the price of one") presidency, implying that Hillary would play an important role in his administration. Early indications from the Clinton White House supported this interpretation. She appointed an experienced staff and set up her own office in the West Wing, an unprecedented move. Her husband appointed her to head the Task Force on National Health Care, a centerpiece of his legislative agenda. She encountered sharp criticism when she closed the sessions of the task force to the public, and doctors and other health care professionals objected that she was not a "government official" and had no right to bar them from the proceedings. An appeals court later supported her stand.

To promote the findings of the task force, she appeared before five congressional committees and received considerable and mostly favorable press coverage for her expertise on the subject. But Congress ultimately rejected the task force's recommendations, and her role in the health care debate galvanized conservatives and helped Republicans recapture Congress in the 1994 elections.

Hillary was criticized on other matters as well, including her role in the firing of seven staff members from the White House travel office ("Travelgate") and her involvement in legal maneuvering by the White House during the Whitewater investigation. As the 1996 election approached, she was less visible and played a more traditional role as first lady. Her first book, *It Takes a Village: And Other Lessons Children Teach Us* (1996), described her views on child rearing and prompted accolades from supporters and stark criticism from her opponents.

Revelations about President Clinton's affair with White House intern Monica Lewinsky brought the first lady back into the spotlight in a complex way. She stood faithfully by her husband during the scandal—in which her husband first denied and then admitted to having had a sexual relationship with Lewinsky—and throughout his ensuing impeachment and trial in the Senate.

In 1999, Hillary made history of a different sort when she launched her candidacy for the U.S. Senate seat from New York. To meet the state's residency requirement, she moved out of Washington, DC, on January 5, 2000, to a house in Chappaqua, New York. After a bitter campaign, she defeated Republican Rick Lazio by a substantial margin to become the first first lady to win elective office. Although often a subject of controversy, Hillary showed that the ceremonial parts of the first lady's job could be merged with a strong role in public policy.

Sworn into office on January 3, 2001, Hillary continued to push for health care reform, and she remained an advocate for children. She served on several senatorial committees, including the Committee for Armed Services. Following the September 11 attacks in 2001, she supported the U.S.-led invasion of Afghanistan but grew highly critical of President George W. Bush's handling of the Iraq War. In 2003, Hillary's much-anticipated memoir of her White House years, *Living History*, was published.

In 2006, Clinton was easily reelected to the Senate. The following year, she announced that she would seek the Democratic Party's presidential nomination for 2008. She ultimately lost the nomination to Barack Obama, who went on to win the general election on November 4, 2008. In December 2008, Obama selected Hillary to serve as secretary of state, and she was confirmed by the Senate in January 2009. Clinton's tenure as secretary of state was widely praised for improving U.S. foreign relationships. She resigned from her post in 2013.

In April 2015, Clinton announced that she was entering the U.S. presidential election race of 2016. Clinton selected Senator Tim Kaine as her vice presidential running mate. On July 26, 2016, at the Democratic National Convention, she was named the party's nominee. Clinton's Republican opponent was Donald Trump, a businessman whose outsider status and political incorrectness had helped him appeal to previously underappreciated voters and secure his party's nomination. As the two candidates faced off, the campaign became increasingly negative and highly acrimonious.

As election day neared, many polls showed Clinton with a sizable lead. Those polls apparently had failed to capture the support enjoyed by Trump in several key Midwestern states, however, and on November 8, 2016, Clinton was defeated in her bid for the presidency; although she won the popular vote by more than 2.8 million, she lost in the electoral college, 227 to 304.

OPRAH WINFREY

(b. Jan. 29, 1954, Kosciusko, Miss., U.S.)

One of the richest and most influential women in the United States is the American television personality, actress, and entrepreneur Oprah Winfrey.

Winfrey moved to Milwaukee, Wisconsin, at age six to live with her mother. In her early teens she was sent to Nashville, Tennessee, to live with her father, who proved to be a positive influence in her life.

At age 19, Winfrey became a news anchor for the local CBS television station. Following her graduation from Tennessee State University in 1976, she was made a reporter and coanchor for the ABC news affiliate in

Oprah Winfrey's syndicated daily talk show was among the most popular of the genre.

Baltimore, Maryland. She found herself constrained by the objectivity required of news reporting. In 1977, she became cohost of the Baltimore morning show *People Are Talking*.

Winfrey excelled in the casual and personal talk-show format, and in 1984 she moved to host the faltering talk show *AM Chicago*. Winfrey's honest and engaging personality quickly turned the program into a success, and in 1985 it was renamed *The Oprah Winfrey Show*. Syndicated nationally in 1986, the program became the highest-rated television talk show in America and earned several Emmy Awards.

In 1985, Winfrey appeared in Steven Spielberg's adaptation of Alice Walker's 1982 novel *The Color Purple*. Her critically acclaimed performance led to other roles. Winfrey formed her own television production company, Harpo Productions Inc. in 1986, and a film production company, Harpo Films, in 1990.

Winfrey broke new ground in 1996 by starting an on-air book club. Each book chosen quickly rose to the top of the bestseller charts. Winfrey further expanded her presence in the publishing industry with the launch of *O, the Oprah Magazine* in 2000 and *O at Home* in 2004.

In 1998, Winfrey expanded her media entertainment empire when she cofounded Oxygen Media, which operates a cable television network for women. The last episode of *The Oprah Winfrey Show* aired in May 2011, and *Oprah's Next Chapter*, a weekly prime-time interview program on the Oprah Winfrey Network (OWN), debuted in January 2012.

Winfrey has engaged in numerous philanthropic activities, including the creation of Oprah's Angel Network, which sponsors charitable initiatives worldwide. In 2007, she opened a $40-million school for disadvantaged girls in South Africa. She is an outspoken crusader against child abuse and has received many honors and awards from civic, philanthropic, and entertainment organizations.

RIGOBERTA MENCHÚ
(b. Jan. 9, 1959, Guatemala)

The Guatemalan Indian-rights activist Rigoberta Menchú was awarded the Nobel Prize for Peace in 1992. Menchú, of the Quiché Maya group, spent her childhood helping with her family's agricultural work. As a young woman, she became an activist in the local women's rights movement and joined with the Catholic church to advocate for social reform.

The activism of Menchú and her family led to persecution by Guatemala's military government. When a guerrilla organization became active in their region, her father, a leader of a peasant organization opposed to the government, was accused of guerrilla activities. During Guatemala's ensuing civil war, he died in a fire while protesting human rights abuses by the military. Menchú's younger brother was kidnapped, tortured, and killed by a military death squad in 1979, and her mother was kidnapped, raped, mutilated, and murdered by soldiers the following year.

Menchú fled to Mexico in 1981 and was cared for there by members of a liberal Roman Catholic group. She soon joined international efforts to make the Guatemalan government cease its brutal counterinsurgency campaigns against Indian peasants, becoming a skilled public speaker and organizer in the course of her efforts.

Menchú gained international prominence in 1983 with her widely translated book *I, Rigoberta Menchú*, in which she tells the story of her impoverished youth and recounts in horrifying detail the torture-murders of her brother and mother. She received the Nobel Peace Prize in 1992 for her continuing efforts to achieve social justice and mutual reconciliation in Guatemala; she used the prize money to found the Rigoberta Menchú Tum Foundation, an Indian advocacy organization. In the late 1990s, her autobiography became the center of controversy after its veracity was questioned, most notably by David Stoll. Despite alleged inaccuracies in her story, Menchú continued to earn praise for bringing international attention to the situation in Guatemala. In 2004, she accepted President Óscar Berger's offer to help implement the country's peace accords.

Menchú created the Indian-led political movement Winaq (Mayan: "The Wholeness of the Human Being") in February 2007. That September, as the candidate of a coalition between Winaq and the left-wing Encounter for Guatemala party, she ran for president of Guatemala but earned less than 3 percent of the vote. Her 2011 presidential bid was also unsuccessful.

DIANA, PRINCESS OF WALES

(b. July 1, 1961, Sandringham, Norfolk, Eng.—d. Aug. 31, 1997, Paris, France)

One of the best-loved women of the 20th century was Diana, princess of Wales, former consort (1981–96) of Charles, prince of Wales (later Charles III), and mother of the heir apparent to the British throne, Prince William.

Diana Frances Spencer was born at Park House, the home that her parents rented on Queen Elizabeth II's estate at Sandringham and where her childhood playmates were the queen's younger sons, Prince Andrew and Prince Edward. She was the third child and youngest daughter of Edward John Spencer, Viscount Althorp, heir to the 7th Earl Spencer, and his first wife, Frances Ruth Burke Roche (daughter of the 4th Baron Fermoy). She became Lady Diana Spencer when her father succeeded to the earldom in 1975. Riddlesworth Hall (near Thetford, Norfolk) and West Heath School (Sevenoaks, Kent) provided the young

Diana's schooling. After attending the finishing school of Chateau d'Oex at Montreux, Switzerland, Diana returned to England and became a kindergarten teacher at the fashionable Young England school in Pimlico.

She renewed her contacts with the royal family, and her friendship with Charles grew in 1980. On February 24, 1981, their engagement was announced, and on July 29, 1981, they were married in Saint Paul's Cathedral in a globally televised ceremony watched by an audience numbering in the hundreds of millions. Their first child, Prince William Arthur Philip Louis of Wales, was born on June 21, 1982, and their second, Prince Henry Charles Albert David, on September 15, 1984. Marital difficulties led to a separation between Diana and Charles in 1992, though they continued to carry out their royal duties and jointly participate in raising their two children. They divorced on August 28, 1996.

After the divorce, Diana maintained her high public profile and continued many of the activities she had earlier undertaken on behalf of charities, supporting causes as diverse as the arts, children's issues, and AIDS patients. Her unprecedented popularity as a member of the royal family attracted considerable attention from the press, and she became one of the most photographed women in the world. Although she used that celebrity to great effect in promoting her charitable work, the media were often intrusive.

It was while attempting to evade journalists that Diana was killed, along with her companion, Dodi Fayed, and their driver, in an automobile accident in a Paris tunnel.

Diana's death and funeral produced unprecedented expressions of public mourning, testifying to her enormous hold on the British national psyche. Her life, and her death, polarized national feeling about the existing system of monarchy (and, in a sense, about the British identity), which appeared antiquated and unfeeling in a populist age of media celebrity, in which Diana herself was a central figure.

Glossary

acrimonious: Angry and bitter.

aegis: Protection, guidance, or control by an individual or group.

autonomous: Existing independently without outside control.

censure: To criticize or blame.

consort: The spouse of royalty.

coup d'état: The sudden overthrow of a government by a small group.

de facto: A Latin phrase meaning "in reality"—e.g., one who has power without officially being in power is a de facto ruler.

epidemiology: A branch of medicine that studies diseases in a population.

guerrilla: Relating to irregular warfare carried out by people outside the military.

prophylactic: Preventing the spread or occurrence of disease or infection.

sterilization: A procedure that makes someone unable to reproduce.

subsidy: A grant given by a government to achieve a result that benefits the public.

suffrage: The right to vote.

For More Information

BOOKS

Adams, Julie, and Louise Wright. *Activists and Leaders*. New York, NY: Gareth Stevens Publishing, 2020.

Clinton, Hillary Rodham, and Chelsea Clinton. *The Book of Gutsy Women: Favorite Stories of Courage and Resilience*. New York, NY: Simon & Schuster, 2019.

Donohue, Caitlin. *She Represents: 44 Women Who Are Changing Politics . . . and the World*. Minneapolis, MN: Zest Books, 2020.

Levy, Janet. *Oprah Winfrey*. New York, NY: Gareth Stevens Publishing, 2021.

WEBSITES

Anne Frank House
www.annefrank.org/en
The official website of the Anne Frank House in Amsterdam contains biographical information, photos, and a virtual tour of the Frank family's secret annex.

Billie Jean King Enterprises
www.billiejeanking.com
This website chronicles Billie Jean King's work for gender equality and highlights her athletic achievements.

The Nobel Prize
www.nobelprize.org
Learn about the prestigious awards presented for world-changing accomplishments and find short biographies of the people—such as Rosalyn Yalow, Nadine Gordimer, Ellen Johnson Sirleaf, Wangari Maathai, Christiane Nüsslein-Volhard, Aung San Suu Kyi, Shirin Ebadi, and Rigoberta Menchú—who won them.

The Royal Family
www.royal.uk
You can find a detailed, multimedia biography of Queen Elizabeth II on the royal family's official website.

INDEX

abortion, 33–34
actors, 6–8, 57–58
AIDS, 37–38, 61
apartheid, 24
Argentina, 19–21
assassinations, 14, 16, 31, 47, 52, 19
athletes, 43–45

Canada, 13, 26–27
cancer, 13–14, 20, 22
China, 10–12, 46
civil rights movement, 8–9
communism, 10–12

disease, 13–14, 22–23, 36

economists, 34–36
England, 21–22, 25–27, 60–61
entrepreneurs, 39–41
environmentalists, 37–39
exile, 20, 24, 31, 35, 51

films, 8, 58
first lady, 52, 54–55

genetics, 21–22, 41–42
Green Belt Movement, 38–39
Guatemala, 59–60

Holocaust, 28–30
human rights, 38–39, 45–51, 59
imprisonment, 10, 12, 17, 35, 41, 51

India, 16–19, 27, 47–48
indigenous rights, 59–60

Iran, 50–51
Ireland, 45–47

judges, 32–35, 50–51

Kenya, 37–39

lawyers, 32–33, 45–46, 50–56
Liberia, 34–36

Netherlands, 28–30
Nicaragua, 31–32
Nobel Prize, 22, 24, 34, 37–38, 41–42, 47
Norway, 36–37

presidents (female), 31–32, 34–36
prime ministers (female), 14–19, 36–37
public health, 13, 36–37

royalty, 25–28, 60–61

scientists, 13–14, 21–24, 41–42
South Africa, 24–25
Sri Lanka, 14–16

talk shows, 57–58
television, 6–8, 40, 53, 57–58
tennis, 43–45

United Nations, 35–38, 45
United States, 6–9, 13, 22–24, 27, 32–35, 38, 43–45, 52–58

writers, 24–25